MW00667113

To: Scott Hudson

Best Wishes

Joe Dye

From Appalachia to the White House

My Life in the Secret Service
Chronicles of the Life of Joe Dye

Joe Dye

CROSSBOOKS
PUBLISHING

CrossBooks™
A Division of LifeWay
1663 Liberty Drive
Bloomington, IN 47403
www.crossbooks.com
Phone: 1-866-879-0502

First published by CrossBooks 6/28/2011

ISBN: 978-1-4627-0516-0 (sc)
ISBN: 978-1-4627-0517-7 (hc)

Library of Congress Control Number: 2011933200

Printed in the United States of America

This book is printed on acid-free paper.

Contents

Dedication

This book is dedicated to my grandson's Luke, Benjamin and Samuel Dye.

Acknowledgements

Thanks to the following for their encouragement and advice during the writing of this book:

To my wife, Sue, who has shown great patience with me thoughout the process of writing my memoirs and she has also kept me on a straight path over the past forty-seven years.

To my sisters, Harriet Cole, Mona Hamm and Lou Emma Jones, who reviewed the manuscript and made suggestions. They also provided some old family photographs.

To Kathy Akers who encouraged me to write this book.

To Linda Martin who reviewed my manuscript and then contacted the publisher in order to get this project underway.

To Jon, Echo and Sam at Crossbooks Publishers, who have guided me though this project.

Introduction

Chronicles Of Joe Leonard Dye

Retired US Secret Service
Uniformed Division

Joe Dye

Today's date is Saturday January 8, 2011. My name is Joe Dye and this is my seventy-first birthday. This occasion reminds me how long I've been on earth and how many adventures I've had, I am eager to share them.

For the past forty-six years, my wife, Sue, and I have made this journey together. The early years of our marriage revolved around our two sons, Timothy and Bradley. It continues today with our three grandsons, Luke, Ben and Sam. Over the years, I have been asked why I haven't written down my life story. I had not felt the urge to do so until my grandsons started asking questions about my life. They wanted to know what things were like in the old days. I originally set out to write my autobiography just for my family so that someone would have a record of my life.

I prepared a draft and asked a friend to review it. After getting my permission, she contacted a publisher, who in turn called me and requested a copy of the manuscript. After reading it, he suggested that we make it into a book.

The farm that we lived on was about thirty-five acres. Some of the property was used for rotating crops, such as corn, potatoes, and tomatoes. Other parts were hilly with trees. We also had cows that grazed on parts of the land. The farm is located on Wysor Valley Road, about five miles from the town of Honaker, Virginia, in Russell County. Today, my first cousins, William Beverly Dye and Earl Harvey Dye, live on the farm. William Beverly, who is now seventy-seven years of age, has lived his entire life on the farm.

The Town of Honaker was originally known as the New Garden settlement. Prior to the name change, the Cherokee and Shawnee Indians roamed the area. Their trails crossed at the mouth of Lewis Creek and Clinch River. The two tribes of Indians did not take lightly to the white man settling in that area. There is a legend of Indians raiding the villages on Big A Mountain and taking captive the women and children while the men were out working the fields or cutting timber. The Indians with their captives headed across the mountains toward Kentucky and Ohio.

When the men returned and found their homes burned and women and children missing they began tracking them. About two days later, they were found near the Kentucky border. The settlers waited until night and took them by surprise and attacked, killing the Indians and rescuing the women and children.

The Indians continued the raids of white villages until 1794 when Chief Benge, a half-breed was killed.

The town began to prosper when Martin Honaker and his sons built grist mills on Lewis Creek and Clinch River. On December 4, 1847, a federal post office was located inside Harvey Honaker's General Store. A short time later the name of the settlement was changed from New Garden to Honaker.

On July 28, 1919, the Town of Honaker was incorporated. The population of the town increased considerably when the Norfolk and Western Railway established a route through it. Timber was the main commerce that brought big companies from the north to come in and buy up large parcels of land. The price of the land at that time was selling for $1.00 per acre. The small town sits among the hills and has little room to expand, making it difficult for industries to locate there. Many young people leave the area after high school to find work. Those that go on to college usually do not return because of the employment situation. Coal mining provided work for the people but that has dwindled to just a small operation now. The lay of the land is so rough that farming is difficult. Most of the farmable land was owned by Stuart Land and Cattle Company of Virginia, which at one time covered over 50,000 acres, and was located in four counties. Today it is still the largest cattle ranch east of the Mississippi River. The Stuart family and farm dates back to Patrick Henry. Also, J.E.B. Stuart, from the American Civil War days, is a cousin of this family. The Stuart Land and Cattle Company's headquarters is located in Rosedale, Virginia, which is 5 miles outside the town of Honaker. Henry C. Stuart was elected and served as Governor of Virginia from 1914 to 1918. (Cary, 2011, April 7). He was born on January 18, 1855, and died on July 24, 1933.

In 1900 the Town of Honaker had a population of 297 people. After the push for timber the population grew. When I left the area in 1958, the population was estimated to be between 600 and 1,000 people. The 1980 census was esatimated to be approximately 1,475. Today the number is about the same.

In 1986 Honaker was declared the Redbud Capitol of the World. In April of each year there is a Redbud Festival in town which draws people from far and near.

Someone traveling to Honaker normally is going for a specific reason because it is off the beaten path. When I travel there today from Roanoke I usually take I-81 south to Christiansburg, Virginia and then go west on Rt. 460 to Princeton, West Virginia. I then take I-77 south to Bluefield and then back onto Rt. 460/Rt.19 to Claypool Hill. Staying on Rt. 19 to Rosedale and turn north on Rt. 80 for 5 miles to Honaker. You can also travel south on I-81 to Wytheville and take I-77 north to Bluefield and then follow the previously described route. You can also continue on I-81 to Abingdon and take Rt. 19 north to Rosedale and north on Rt. 80 into Honaker. So you see one usually has a specific purpose when traveling to Honaker.

When I first lived in Washington, D.C. there were no Interstate highways and it took about 12 hours to travel to Honaker. Now that there are Interstate highways, it takes about 7 hours.

Chapter 1

My Family History

My father, Clarence Sheffey Dye was born August 8, 1902, in Honaker. He died on January 10, 1957, at the age of fifty-four. He was the son of Beverly Fuller Dye and Mary Randolf Johnson Dye.

Grandmother Mary Johbnson Dye and
Grandfather Beverly F. Dye

My father worked his entire adult life for the Norfolk and Western Railway. He worked most of his career as a brakeman for the railroad. About a year before his death, he received a promotion to be a conductor. This position placed him in charge of the freight train to which he was assigned. Working for the railroad was considered one of the best jobs a person living in southwest Virginia could have. My father enjoyed his work, but often said that he did not want to see his boys continuing in his footsteps because it required being out in all kinds of weather and the work was dangerous.

My father never completed high school, but he taught me many lessons. To me, it seemed that he could solve any problem. One lesson that stands out the most was that you should always do your best at whatever you do. Doing your best meant that you would not have to do a job that would create double work. It also meant that you had the satisfaction of giving your best to the job. He also set an excellent example of being a Christian.

During World War I, my father was too young to serve in the army—and by the time World War II came along, he was too old to serve. He also had a lot of mouths to feed. I recall my father mentioning unkind words about two people: Hitler and Tojo. These people did not mean much to me except that they were our country's enemies. He really wanted to do his part for the war effort. He turned in scrap metal so it could be made into weapons for the war.

My father's work was quite interesting and there are a few stories I would like to share about him. In the early 1940s, when I was about two years old, he was involved in a train derailment in West Virginia. He was seriously burned on his arms and hands from the steam coming from the engine. At that time, the railroad only had steam engines. It wasn't until the mid 1950s that diesel engines came into use. My sister Harriet gave me the information about the derailment since I was too young to remember the details.

In the late 1940s, he was in another accident at Weller Yard, which is located near Grundy, Virginia. This accident happened while switching railcars at night. He was struck from behind by another train and knocked down between the tracks. The train continued traveling over him for a long distance before they could stop it. The cuts and bruises he received over his entire body caused him to miss work for a few weeks.

Harriet drove to Grundy to bring him home and I remember seeing him painfully limp into the house.

In 1956, on another train, a man was killed when he was hit by the train while lying with his head on the track. When the engineer saw him, he blew the whistle and applied the brakes, but he could not stop the train. It takes anywhere from half a mile to more than a mile to stop a loaded train when traveling at fifty miles per hour. It was determined later that the man was intoxicated and had passed out. When the accident happened, my father was the conductor and riding in the caboose. The caboose is a thing of the past since the 1970s when railroads were allowed to discontinue their use.

After the engineer got the train stopped, my father had to walk back to the scene to find out what had happened. He had to file accident reports with the railroad and law enforcement. He also had to testify before an inquiry board. He was shaken about the incident and was extremely concerned about the dead man's family. About six months later, my father died from a massive heart attack while he was on vacation. My father had been working all morning on the farm with my brother Stanley. They were repairing the old house that our family had lived in so that Stanley and his family could move into it. At about noon, he told my brother and my grandfather that he was not feeling well and he drove back to our house in Honaker. After lunch, he did not return to the farm. He was on the couch in the living room and my mother was checking on him often. She sat next to him and put his head on her lap. My mother said that, shortly thereafter, my father's body gave a big jerk and he went limp. He died with his head on her lap.

I was in my junior year of high school when my father passed away. During basketball practice after school, the school secretary came to the gym and advised me that I was needed at home because my father was sick. She drove me home and on the way we met an ambulance. She said everything must be all right because they did not have the emergency lights on.

When I arrived home, I learned that my father had died. I was in shock because I had never thought that anything like this would happen. Other than the accidents, my father never even used sick leave. After the funeral, it dawned on me that my mother would have a difficult time because there were still four kids in school. It played a big part in my decision to not accept a scholarship offer to play basketball in college. My father is buried in Russell Memorial Cemetery in Lebanon, Virginia.

My mother, Hazel Emma Settle Dye, was born on April 14, 1909, in the Elk Garden area of Russell County. She died on August 13, 2001, at the age of ninety-two. In 1955, my mother was appointed as the postmaster of the Putnam, Virginia, post office. Since I had just gotten my driver's license, she would have me drive to the post office and build a fire in the woodstove. When she arrived, the small building would be warm. She certainly enjoyed the job at the post office and looked forward to getting out of the house and meeting other people. She was disappointed when the post office closed two years later.

During my high school days, she started to substitute teach at Honaker High School. She worked these jobs to supplement the cost of raising a large family. She was the daughter of Marion Hix Settle and Loudema Williams Jones Settle.[1]

My parents had ten children. They are:

- Mary Williams Dye: She was born on May 4, 1929, and she died from pneumonia on October 3, 1935. She is buried in the Johnson Cemetery on Wysor Valley Road.
- Harriet Fern Dye Cole: She was born on March 1, 1931, and she lives in Cedar Bluff, Virginia.
- Mona Annette Dye Hamm: She was born on November 11, 1932, and she lives in Cedar Bluff.
- Clarence Stanley Dye: He was born on February 2, 1935 and died on January 1, 1986. He is buried in Greenhills Memory Gardens Cemetery in Claypool Hill, Virginia.

1 Whitt, Mollie Settle. "History of Marion Hix Settle." The Heritage of Russell County Virginia 1786–1986, vol. 1. Salem, WV: Don Mills, Inc., 1985, 311–312.

- Carl Herman Dye: He was born on May 10, 1936, and died on September 22, 1996. He is buried in Greenhills Memory Gardens Cemetery.
- Mildred Alice Dye Carpenter: She was born on November 20, 1937, and lives in Waldorf, Maryland.
- Joe Leonard Dye: He was born on January 8, 1940, and lives in Roanoke, Virginia.
- Nancy Sue Dye Mason: She was born on August 3, 1941, and lives in San Antonio, Texas.
- James Douglas Dye: He was born on March 17, 1945, and lives in Waldorf.
- Lou Emma Dye Jones: She was born on March 18, 1946, and lives in Fredericksburg, Virginia.

Hazel & Clarence with Mary Williams

Clarence on bycicle

Hazel & Clarence

During our family gatherings, my mother would tell us about events from the past. When she was about eighty years old, she told us about when she and our father were married. In 1927, when she was eighteen and my father was twenty-five, they decided to elope. Without their parents' knowledge, she skipped school and they drove in my father's pickup truck to Bristol, Virginia, where they were married by the justice of the peace. Since they did not have the money to pay him, my father took a crate of chickens as payment. They lived with their families for about six months before telling them that they were married.

My mother had difficulty telling this story because she was laughing so hard. She said that rumors began to circulate, but her mother said, "My Hazel would not do such a thing." I checked with my older sisters and they said that they had never heard that story before. She loved to tell us stories about our family—no matter how wonderful or terrible they were.

I was twenty-six and my mother was fifty-seven years when she took her first airplane ride. My brother-in-law, Gerald Carpenter, and I flew a single-engine Cessna 172 from the Washington, D. C. area to Richlands, Virginia, where my mother was living. After picking up my mother at the airport, we flew her back to Washington for a visit with family members living in the D.C. area. The windy day created a rough ride.

On the return flight, I had to land in Bluefield, West Virginia, to refuel. Under normal circumstances, I could make the roundtrip flight without refueling, but the strong headwinds caused us to use more fuel than normal. We did not have enough fuel to make it back to Washington without stopping. When they built Bluefield Airport, they leveled the top of a mountain and the runway came out to the edge of the mountain where it drops off. The wind was extremely gusty and I made probably the worse landing I had ever made. I had to come in faster than normal and the plane bounced a few times before settling onto the runway.

After taxiing to the terminal, the tower radioed me to advise that they were out of fuel. I decided that I had enough fuel to fly to Roanoke for refueling. I was cleared to taxi back to the runway for takeoff, but just as I reached the active runway, the tower advised me that the fuel truck was just arriving at the airport. I returned to the terminal and waited until my plane was refueled. The trip back to Washington was very rough and I thought my mother would never fly again. To my surprise, she thoroughly enjoyed the flight. From that time on, she flew often. She even took a flight to Hawaii.

As my mother became elderly, her health became poor. When she developed Parkinson's disease, my sister Mona had her come to live with her until her death. Our entire family was very happy that Mona volunteered to take care of her during her remaining years. My mother loved Mona and her husband, Jack. The three of them got along well. It was very hard to see my mother's health deteriorate. She also had a hiatal hernia that made it very difficult to swallow food. She could only eat baby food for the last few years of her life. Through all of this, my mother never lost her sense of humor.

My middle name, Leonard, is the name of my mother's brother. I never knew anything about him until I was fifteen years old and he was killed in an automobile accident in Montana. It turns out that he was an outlaw. The story goes that, while my uncle and some other young men were walking down a road near their home laughing and making lots of noise, a man with a bad temper came out of his house and threatened them with a gun. My uncle went home, got a gun, and returned to the scene. An argument ensued and my uncle shot and killed the man. The police set up roadblocks for him, but he was able to escape with the help of a neighbor. The neighbor was driving him out of the area when they came upon one of the roadblocks. My uncle jumped out of the vehicle before they got to the roadblock and somehow was able to leave the state.

I remember a few occasions when a stranger would show up at our house late at night. No one would say who he was, but I learned later that it was Uncle Leonard. After he died, I learned that he had changed his name to Freeman and had been living in Montana for years and working in the silver mines. I was fifteen years old when he was brought back and buried in Russell Memorial Cemetery in Lebanon, Virginia. My parents said that the police did not pursue the case because it was possible that he killed the man in self-defense—plus the man had been a problem in the neighborhood for years.

I never knew my Grandfather Settle. He died before I was born. All I remember about my Grandmother Settle was that when our family visited my Aunt Lilly Hankins, where my grandmother was living, my Grandmother Settle usually was in bed. She was a large woman with diabetes and was in poor health.

Since my grandmother on my father's side of the family died when I was about one year old, I cannot remember her.

When I was in the second grade, my Grandfather Dye was living in a small trailer near Oak Ridge, Tennessee. He was working on a construction job that turned out to be the Oak Ridge Nuclear Plant, but he came home on some weekends. I was seven years old when his job was completed and he moved back to the farm with the trailer.

My grandfather had lived in the trailer since his house had burned eight years earlier. I was nine years old when he started renovating an old storage building on the property and made a two-room living quarters for himself. It consisted of a kitchen and one bedroom. He installed a wood-burning cook stove before finishing the other parts. He had not installed the glass windows yet. After cooking his meals on the stove, he washed the dishes and pans with soapy water. With one motion, he threw the water out the window. He did this one day, but forgot that he had installed the windows. The dishpan struck the window with such force that it broke the glass. I came by a little later and my grandfather laughed and made a teaching lesson out of the situation.

The bedroom consisted of a big featherbed that I loved to sink into. It was easy to be swallowed up in that big feather mattress. There was a potbelly wood stove to heat the room, and a couple of straight back chairs. A tin can filled with water on the stove would give off steam to create humidity in the room.

He was so gentle and patient with all of us kids. I always enjoyed his teaching me how to make things from scrap metal and just ordinary work on the farm.

He also had a sense of humor. Each year after cutting the hay, we would put it in stacks. All the kids from the neighborhood liked to jump on the haystacks, which would scatter the hay. My grandfather slipped a few thistles in the hay and boy what a shock it was to us when we jumped on the haystack. My brother Herman helped my grandfather put the thistles in the hay and then he suggested that we all go jump on the hay. He stayed back and laughed at us as we cried out in pain.

My mother really had a difficult time raising all her children, but she never complained. My older sisters, Harriet, Mona, and Millie, had a big responsibility for helping raise us younger children. Everyone had to pitch in and help. They washed the clothes and hung them on an outside clothesline to dry. My mother prepared at least three meals each day. Our dining table was a long, homemade table with benches down two sides and chairs at each end that were understood to be for my father and mother.

My mother would always see that we were in church on Sundays. In getting everyone ready, she could get frustrated with one of us and start at the top of the list, rapidly reciting the names of her children until she got to the one being chastised. This could happen at other times also. As I have gotten older—even with just two sons and three grandsons—I understand why my mother had to go down the list to get to the right person.

During the summer, we seldom wore shoes. We had a great time running many miles on the cow paths of the hills with a lid from a lard can, pretending it was the steering wheel of a coal truck. When we got tired, we would run slow and say we were saving gas.

When my father died, my mother still had four children in school. I don't know how she was able to handle this situation, but somehow she did with the help of God.

Grandfather Dye had a second stroke after I graduated from high school, and my mother cared for him in her home until he passed away. He was born on December 4, 1877, and I was twenty-two when he died on March 26, 1962, at the age of eighty-five. He is buried in the Johnson Cemetery.

Beverly F. Dye

My mother is buried in Russell Memorial Cemetery in Lebanon, Virginia. I know she has received many crowns in heaven.

Chapter 2

My Childhood Life

I was born in my parent's home on January 8, 1940. There was a heavy snowstorm and my father walked about two miles from our home on Wysor Valley Road to Dr. Cox's home in Putnam, Virginia, a small community located between Honaker and Wysor Valley. Dr. Cox and my father proceeded to our house on horseback where he assisted with my birth.

House where Joe was born

Joe at 2 years of age

Later, my mother would laugh at the fact that Dr. Cox signed my birth certificate on the line for the father's signature. It was not noticed until later, and the birth certificate had to be changed.

When I was three, our house (pictured above) caught fire and burned to the ground. Before the fire, my father had already begun building another house on the property for us to live in.

When I was four, my parents noticed that I had difficulty keeping up with other children while playing and I fell a lot when running. After consulting with doctors, they learned that one of my legs was about one and a half inches longer than the other. A decision was made for my father to take me by train across the state to Children's Hospital of Richmond. I remained there for thirteen months while physical therapy was performed on my legs. About once a month, my father would bring one of my brothers or sisters to visit.

During my stay in the hospital, another boy and I would find unused wheelchairs in the hallway. We would race each other down the hallways until a nurse stopped us. Back then, the wheelchairs were big and heavy—not like the ones today. On the day that I was released from the hospital, tears of joy flowed down my cheeks for the thought of going home. The train left the station in Richmond and headed for southwest Virginia. Afterward, I returned to Richmond every six months for therapy until my legs were the same length.

When I entered first grade, I wore a brace with a built-up shoe on one leg and foot—and walked with crutches. Eventually I was able to discard the crutches, but I walked with the brace and shoe for five years.

When I was nine, my father was having a problem with the battery in his pickup truck. He would park it on a hill near our barn so that he could let it drift off. As it was rolling down the hill, he would put it in gear and let the clutch out, causing the engine to turn over and start.

My two older brothers, Stanley and Herman, were inside the pickup pretending to drive it. They would change gears and turn the steering wheel while making sounds of a vehicle. I was about twenty feet away when they got out of the vehicle. They had left the gearshift in neutral and released the emergency brake. A short time later, I noticed the truck beginning to move. I ran, opened the passenger door, and jumped in. I tried to stop the truck, but it was going down a fairly steep embankment. The open door struck an apple tree and broke the window; the truck continued until it hit a fence. My two brothers scurried behind my grandfather's house and hid as my father came running. After seeing I was not injured—but before finding out what had happened—he gave me a real spanking (in other words, a whipping). I did not have time to explain and my brothers did not come to my defense.

Years later, my mother told me that my father found out what had happened and felt badly about giving me the spanking. He told her that I did not say a word; I just stood there and took the spanking.

I remember wonderful times growing up in Wysor Valley. When I was very young, there were several families in our neighborhood.

These families included my family, my cousins, W. B. and Earl Harvey Dye, the Hess boys, C. A., Ulysses, and Sherman, the Perkins boys, the Deskins, and others. We made up games to play and there was always competition between us.

At Christmas, our church would have the children recite the Christmas story. Afterward, there was always a brown paper bag filled with candy and fruit that my father had provided for all the kids in the church. Even though we did not have a lot of money, my father made sure that each of his children had a gift for Christmas.

I recall some winters when we had large snowstorms as big as when I was born. My mother was concerned that the children might fall into a snowdrift, of which we had many, and they would not be able to find us. I remember playing in the snow when it was above our heads. We learned that, by digging tunnels in the snow, it was warmer inside because you were shielded from the wind. As always, there were lots of snowball fights and we would pile up the snow and make forts to hide behind.

Sorghum Molasses

Up until fourth grade, all of the neighbors came together to cut the sugarcane and make sorghum molasses each fall. We would plant lots of sugarcane in the spring of the year, and by late summer—when the stalks were full of juice—they would be cut and stripped of their leaves. The stalks would be gathered and brought to a grinding machine. The grinding machine was made of two large cylinders that were against each other and attached to a long wooden pole that extended about twelve feet to turn the cylinders.

A horse that was hitched to the pole would walk in a circle. Someone would sit on the ground with a large amount of sugarcane stalks that were fed between the two cylinders. As the cylinders turned, it would squeeze the juice out of the stalks. The juice would drain into a large pan. Another large metal pan about ten feet by six feet and about one foot deep would be placed nearby with lots of wood for a fire underneath the pan. The juice was poured into the pan and the fire was started. The juice would be constantly stirred as it came to a boil. The foam would be skimmed off and the juice would be stirred until it turned into sorghum molasses. This process usually lasted all day and night, but if there was a large amount of sugarcane, it could take days to complete the task.

My responsibilities consisted of feeding the stalks into the grinder, removing the ground up stalks, and keeping wood available for the fire. There would be several neighborhood boys rotating on these jobs. We needed to be aware of the long pole being pulled by the horse and duck each time it passed over us or risk getting a knot on our head.

When I was nine years old, we did not have a horse to pull the pole and turn the grinder. My father had a pickup truck with a steering wheel that could be locked in place. He was able to lock the steering wheel in a position that allowed it to go around the grinder at the same distance. The truck's throttle could be set at a slow pace. After it was going, my dad would step out of the truck and let it continue around without anyone in the truck.

The women and girls had the hard task of cleaning the pots and pans used during this process. They also were responsible for putting the molasses in mason jars and sealing them. Since this was a community project, everyone received their share of the molasses.

Hog Killing Time

Until my family moved to town in 1949, Thanksgiving was always a very busy time on the farm. Cold weather usually had set in and it was hog killing time. Everyone had jobs to do. Since we did not have refrigerators or freezers, all the meat had to be taken care of as soon as possible. Nothing was thrown away. My mother would grind the sausage—and then it had to be cooked and canned. We would have several half-gallon jars filled with sausage. Lard was heated and poured around the meat in the jars and then they were sealed. When the lard cooled, it turned white and become solid. The hams had to be cured and put in the smokehouse. We had no running water in our house and had to carry it from the spring. Milk and butter were kept in a springhouse that was built over the stream of water coming from the spring. A wooden box with a lid was placed in the water for milk, butter, and other things that needed to be kept cool.

We did not have electricity in our house until I was three years old. Even after electricity was available to the area, there was one family in the valley that refused to let the power company run the power lines through their property. This delayed the rest of the families in the valley from getting electricity for almost a year. My father had our house wired for electricity months prior to the electric company getting the power lines in and the electricity turned on. The children liked to run through the house and we had a habit of flipping the light switches as we went. I remember how surprised we were one day when we flipped a switch and the light came on for the first time.

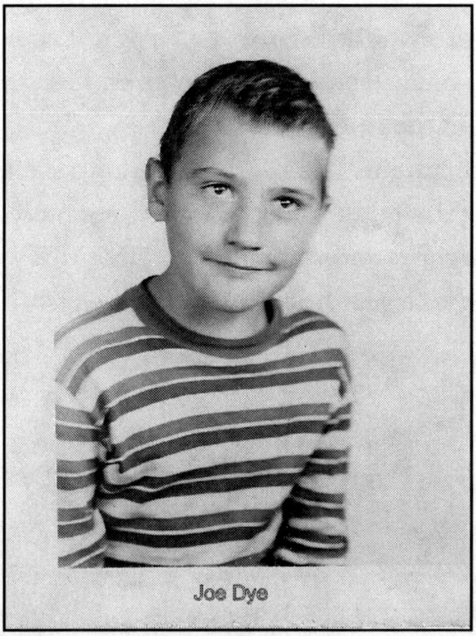

Joe's 4th grade picture

During fourth grade, my family purchased a house in the Cox Town section of Honaker. We moved from the farm to the new house in Honaker where I lived until graduation from high school.

Honaker High School and Honaker Elementary School shared the same building until I was in the fifth grade. A new high school was built on a lot adjacent to the old building and the elementary school remained in the old one. There was not a middle school and seventh grade was considered the freshman class. A coal-fired furnace produced steam for the radiators and heated the school.

In elementary school, the boys were mischievous and did anything to get out of school. One such incident happened when I was in the fourth grade. Somebody caught a skunk and cut its scent bag out. They brought the scent bag to school and placed it under a radiator. When the heat caused it to burst, the entire school was closed for several days until the scent was gone. I am not aware that the school officials ever found out who did it.

After moving to Honaker, I also remember playing with Ronnie Musick, Sherman Compton, Larry Wysor, Robert Bowman, and others. During the summer, we went to the ball field at the old Honaker High School and played baseball all day long. Our parents didn't worry about us then the way that parents do today because of the crime situation. Larry Wysor was a little younger, but we spent a lot of time playing at his house. In good weather, we played baseball or basketball at Larry's house. If it was raining, we played in their barn or underneath the bridge that crossed Lewis Creek.

Chapter 3

My Teen Years

Ronnie, Sherman, and I played on the Honaker High School baseball and basketball teams. The three of us were best friends. Sherman was a gentle giant. He was six foot seven and one of the kindest persons I have ever known. After college, Sherman became a schoolteacher and coach. He passed away several years ago and is sorely missed today, especially by his wife Shirley and his family.

Since Ronnie's family owned a TV set and we didn't, he often invited me over to watch "Gillette Friday Night Boxing." After the theater burned in Honaker and we had our driver's licenses, our parents occasionally let us use their cars to go to the movies in Lebanon or Richlands.

During high school, I encountered a few incidents that I'm not proud of. In my senior year, there were about four of us boys—I will not mention their names—that decided to skip school and drive to Bluefield, Virginia, for the day. Unbeknownst to the four of us, there were about thirty other students that skipped school that same day and went to South Holston Lake and Abingdon, Virginia. The next day, the principal announced over the speaker system a list of names with instructions for them to report to his office. When Mr. Baldwin started reciting the names, the four of us began sliding down in our seats. We were waiting for our names to be called because we had been informed earlier in the day about the others who had skipped school the same day we did. Someone had seen them and reported it to the principal. All of those students were suspended from school for three days. Needless to say, we did not say a word about us skipping school.

After I graduated from high school, I met Mr. Baldwin at a service station and told him about the incident. I asked why we were not called to the office that day. He said that he was not aware that the four of us had skipped school—but if he had, we would have been suspended also. I am sorry that I did not put more effort into my studies during high school. I would have been better prepared for college if I had.

I've been to several of our high school class reunions and have enjoyed the fellowship with my classmates. The last reunion was our fiftieth.

We had a small tobacco allotment from the government to raise tobacco. It was a big job in early spring before the frost free date to prepare a seedbed. We burned off the area to kill any weeds. The tobacco seeds were sown in the bed and a cheesecloth covering was placed over it to keep the frost out. After the weather warmed up, we took off the covers. The seed came up as small tobacco plants. When it came time to plant the tobacco, we pulled up just enough plants that could be planted that day. The work didn't stop with the planting. We busied ourselves hoeing the ground, keeping the worms off the leaves, suckering the little sprouts that grew out of the stalk by the leaves, and breaking off the tops when they began making seed pods. When it was time to cut the tobacco, it would be put on stakes about four feet long and hauled to the barn where it was hung to dry. By Thanksgiving, it was usually time to get the tobacco down from the barn and start grading the leaves. After grading the leaves, small bundles were tied with another leaf and placed by its grade. After all the grading and tying, the entire crop was taken to the tobacco auction in Abingdon, Virginia. After the sale was completed, my father received a check in the mail for the amount due him. This was our Christmas money. Usually it was used to buy clothes for the kids. We were poor by worldly standards, but we didn't know it because everyone else was in the same boat.

We continued to use the farm to grow crops for food. When I was fourteen, my father bought a farm tractor. He used to let me sit in his lap while he worked with the tractor. He taught me how to change the equipment, such as the plows, disk hire, mowers, and hay rakes. Later, he allowed me to use the tractor to plow gardens for our neighbors and cut their hay along with doing the work on our farm. This was a way that I could earn spending money. It made me feel good when people would make comments about what a good job I had done plowing their garden or cutting their hay.

My grandfather continued to live on the farm, but when I was in high school he had a light stroke. My parents asked me to stay with him at night so that he wouldn't be alone. I rode the bus to school and was involved in sports after school. I then walked back to my grandfather's house in Wysor Valley.

The school system required only eleven grades to complete high school. Two years after I graduated, the system changed to the twelve grade requirement.

God still performs miracles. Even with the earlier problems with my legs, I made the Honaker High School varsity basketball and baseball teams. I played both sports all four years of high school. I enjoyed playing the two sports that the high school offered. I was successful in both games and was voted most athletic in our school's yearbook. I was offered, but declined, a scholarship to play basketball at Marshall University in Huntington, West Virginia. I felt that I needed to get a job and not be a burden to my mother. My grades in high school were not the best and I had concerns about being able to keep up with the academics in college, but I had no doubt that I could play ball on the college level.

Chapter 4

My First Jobs

My first jobs were during high school when I worked part time in a grocery store and a service station. After graduating from high school, I borrowed money to move to Winston-Salem, North Carolina, with Ronnie Musick. The only work I could find there was in a service station. After working through the summer, Ronnie and I moved to Richmond, Virginia. Neither of us had money so the landlord of another person we knew let us stay in her boarding house and fed us until we got jobs.

Ronnie and I both got jobs with Philip Morris Tobacco Company. I worked in the shipping department and Ronnie was assigned to keep the machines running. Ronnie had previously applied for a job with the General Electric Company in Bucyrus, Ohio. When he received an offer from them, he moved there to take the job. Ronnie and I have stayed in touch over the years and remain the best of friends.

Federal Bureau of Investigation (FBI)

FBI Director J. Edgar Hoover

While I was working in Richmond, my sister Millie was employed with the FBI in Washington. She persuaded me to apply for a job there.

Joe – FBI Basketball

I was twenty years old when I placed an application with the FBI Richmond Field Office. I was hired for a position in the Communications Division at FBI Headquarters in Washington. My assignment was in the mailroom where we processed all the mail coming in and going out. We had a special section where mail going to United State embassies around the world was processed. These required special tamper-proofing procedures. I was also required to hand-carry special letters from Mr. Hoover to the White House and to congressmen and senators at the United States Capitol building. Director Hoover was a big supporter of the FBI basketball and baseball teams that played in the Washington Industrial League. Our baseball games were played on either the Washington Monument grounds or the Ellipse, located south of the White House. I made both teams. I played third base for our baseball team and, for two years, I had a batting average above .400. The Washington Senators baseball team (now the Minnesota Twins) invited me to try out for their team. I spent three days with them before I was cut. As I look back, I take solace because the guy that beat me out was Harmon Killebrew; he is now in the Baseball Hall of Fame.

The FBI had good baseball teams because Mr. Hoover made sure that the best players were assigned to the Washington area. Sometime after I left the FBI, a special agent complained to his congressman that Mr. Hoover was showing favoritism to the baseball players by assigning them to the Washington Field Office or Headquarters. Mr. Hoover then decided to discontinue the sponsorship of sports teams.

Vic Turyn was the FBI Special Agent in Charge (SAC) of the St. Louis Field Office. Vic was an All-American quarterback for the University of Maryland in the late 1940s. I met Vic through my supervisor, John J. O'Keefe. Most times that Vic returned to Washington for meetings, John and I would have lunch with him. He suggested that I transfer to the St. Louis office and work with him. My transfer was approved, but before I made the move, I made the mistake of sending material to the special agent (or "legal attaché," as he was called) working in the US Embassy in Buenos Aries when the material should have gone to the agent in the US Embassy in London. I also had material going to the agent in London. I mistakenly switched the mailing labels on the two packages. The agent in London covered for me by sending the package directly to Buenos Aires, but the agent in Buenos Aires sent the package back to Washington and I received a letter of reprimand from Mr. Hoover for my mistake.

When you messed up at the FBI, you were either fired or transferred to the Butte Field Office. Butte, Montana, was the graveyard for FBI employees. The assistant director of the communications division called me in to discuss the situation. Afterward, along with my supervisor, we were shocked that my punishment would be merely the cancellation of my transfer to St. Louis. Instead of exile in Butte, I was to remain at headquarters in Washington! I think Mr. Hoover took pity on this old country boy because that usually did not happen within the Bureau.

Employees of the Bureau, when approaching Mr. Hoover, would give him a wide berth. Stories floated around that if he did not like the way you presented yourself, you didn't stay around long. I guess that I was so naive that when we approached each other, I would always speak to him and he would speak to me.

In December 1961, I resigned from the FBI to take a position as a policeman on the Metropolitan Police Department. Mr. Hoover called me to his office, and we had a long conversation. He wished me well and told me to contact him if I ever needed anything.

Chapter 5

My Wife and Children

All things have a purpose in life. I would not have met and married Sue Harper if the incident with Mr. Hoover had not occurred.

Sue Harper Dye

I was twenty one years old and working for the FBI when I met the most beautiful young lady from Ellijay, Georgia. I tell people that J. Edgar Hoover was the one that brought Sue Harper and me together. Sue worked on the FBI switchboard, which was located just across the hall from Mr. Hoover's office. At that time, the federal buildings in Washington did not have the security that is in place today. Anyone could just enter the buildings and walk the hallways—except for certain restricted areas. People with mental problems often came in wanting to see Mr. Hoover. Since the ladies working the switchboard came in before most of the other workers, Mr. Hoover was concerned for their safety. He wanted a man there to protect them; at twenty-one years of age, I was assigned the duty.

Sue and I struck up a casual conversation and, after several days, I finally got up enough nerve to ask her to lunch. She agreed and I guess you can say we had our first date over lunch in a restaurant on Pennsylvania Avenue across from the FBI building. After several of these luncheons, I finally asked Sue if she would go to a movie with me. Sue loved bowling and we spent time at bowling alleys and youth activities associated with the church. We also loved to have picnics at Fort Washington, overlooking the Potomac River and George Washington's home, Mount Vernon, on the other side.

Millie also worked on the FBI switchboard and I guess she was trying to get Sue and me together. Millie would tell Sue that she was concerned about her younger brother who was single and did not know anyone in Washington. After several of these attempts, Sue asked Millie what her brother's name was. Since Millie's married name was Carpenter, Sue did not know that we were brother and sister. After the shock of learning that we were siblings, Sue told Millie that she didn't have to worry about her brother. She went on to tell her that we had been dating for some time.

After a couple years of dating, our relationship became serious. When marriage came up, I began to get cold feet or was plain scared. We decided that we needed some time alone and our relationship cooled.

Over the next couple years, we were preoccupied with our respective jobs and churches, but our paths crossed from time to time.

By this time, Sue had resigned from the FBI to take a job as a secretary for Metropolitan Baptist Church. About two years after our breakup, I resigned from the FBI to take the policeman job. Luck would have it that I was assigned to the fifth precinct where Sue lived. I called Sue to let her know where I was assigned and we met at Sherrill's Bakery and Restaurant located on the corner of 3rd Street and Pennsylvania Avenue. We had always liked going there for doughnuts and coffee. After that, we talked to each other often and decided to start dating again. About four years after we met, I asked Sue to marry me. I was twenty-four and Sue was twenty-two at the time of our marriage.

Joe & Sue's wedding

We have been married for forty-six years and have two sons (Timothy Leonard Dye and Bradley Stephen Dye). Both live in the Roanoke, Virginia, area. Timothy and his wife, Amy, have three sons (Luke, Benjamin, and Samuel), who are the joy of our lives.

Bradley and his wife, Melissa.

Brad & Missy

Amy, Sam, Tim, Luke & Ben

Timothy was born on October 26, 1967, at Sibley Hospital in Washington. We had just bought our first house in Dale City, Virginia and had to drive thirty miles into Washington for his birth. Sue was in labor most of the night and the hospital staff told me to get some rest because it would be some time before she gave birth. I left and went to the White House for a while. After returning to the hospital, I was informed that she was giving birth at that time. We didn't know what the sex of the baby was before birth. All we prayed for was that it would be healthy—and he was.

Bradley was born on October 9, 1969, at Fairfax Hospital in Fairfax, Virginia. Again, we did not know the sex of this child until birth. Thank the Lord that both were born healthy.

When our boys were growing up, every emergency with them seemed to come when I was out of town on assignment with the Secret Service. Sue ended up by herself at Fairfax Hospital a few times with these emergencies. Brad once fell against the fireplace, causing a large cut on his head which required stitches. She was with Brad a couple times when he stuck a vitamin or an acorn up his nose. Brad had a thing about putting things in his nose. He did this again with a vitamin, but Sue learned that she could squirt water in his nose to dissolve the vitamin. All of these emergencies happened when I was away and Sue ended up having to handle them. When we moved to Roanoke, Virginia, Timothy was going into high school and Bradley was in junior high. After they graduated from William Byrd High School, Tim enrolled at Virginia Tech and Brad went to Virginia Western Community College. After Brad graduated with an associate degree, he enrolled at Virginia Tech. They were together at Virginia Tech for two years and they both graduated with business degrees. Tim is now employed by *Laker Magazine,* which is part of *The Roanoke Times*. Brad is employed with Advance Auto Parts at their headquarters in Roanoke.

We are fortunate to have all our family located close by where we see them often. We especially like having our three grandsons close. All are special to us.

Chapter 6

My Life as a Policeman

Joe – Metropolitan Policeman

After my orientation with the Metropolitan Police Department in Washington, I was assigned to the fifth precinct, which covered the area from the US Capitol Building down East Capitol Street to the Anacostia River, south along the Anacostia River to South Capitol Street, and north on South Capitol Street back to the US Capitol Building. The football stadium, now named RFK (Robert F. Kennedy), was built in the fifth precinct. While I was assigned there, I worked most of the Washington Redskins football games, and Washington Senator's baseball games. The fifth precinct was the smallest, but one of the busiest, precincts in Washington. Eighth Street, SE, was the roughest due to all its bars. The precinct also included the Marine Barracks, located at 8th and I Streets, SE, and the navy yard between South Capitol Street and 11th Street, SE, and from the Anacostia River to M Street, SE.

After being assigned to the fifth precinct, I received further training with experienced officers. I worked with these experienced officers on foot beats, patrol cars, transport wagons, and station duties. I was on the midnight shift the first time I was assigned a foot beat on my own. At one o'clock in the morning, while walking my beat, I heard someone loudly cursing. I noticed a man chasing a group of men and women down the street. He was threatening to kill all of them as they ran into a house. It looked like he had a rifle and he followed them inside.

I ran after them, but they entered the house before I got there. I drew my revolver and kicked the door open. As I entered the room, the man with the rifle had six people lined up against a wall and was still threatening to kill them. He turned and pointed the rifle at me, but did not say anything. I ordered him to put the gun down, but he just mumbled and kept the gun pointed at me. It was the first time that I had looked down the barrel of a gun pointed at me, but I did not have time to think of what could have happened. I kept ordering him to put the gun down. This went on for about fifteen minutes before he decided to put the gun down.

After arresting the man, I checked the rifle and found twenty-one bullets in the magazine and one in the chamber. Since we did not have radios then and there were no phones in the house, I gave my call box key to one of the other people in the room and directed him to the nearest police call box to have a police wagon respond to the scene. After questioning those he had been threatening, I returned to the precinct to make a police report and then went back to my beat. The man was turned over to the detectives for questioning.

About two hours later, I was walking my beat when I heard someone coming down the street whistling. It was the same man! When I questioned him, he said the detectives had let him go. I took him to a call box to check with the station and was advised that the brother of the man, who the detectives knew, came to the station and they released him to his brother. The case never went to court and that was discouraging to me.

While attending the police academy, we took a field trip to the morgue to witness an autopsy. Upon entering the morgue, we were advised that the stench can be unbearable. They kept a large container of Vick's salve for anyone wishing to put some under their nose. The autopsy we witnessed that day was of a woman's body that had been recovered from the Anacostia Rriver. The coroner estimated that the body had been in the water for about a week. When they cut into the bloated body, a big gush of gas was released. Witnessing an autopsy is eye opening, but it helps to understand what a coroner looks for to determine a death. It also helps to understand the testimony of the coroner during a trial. I'll spare you the gruesome details of seeing a body being cut open and the skull being opened with a power saw.

After graduating from the police academy, I had the opportunity to witness several other autopsies. The morgue was located in the fifth precinct and I would often stop in and watch them perform autopsies while I was working the midnight shift.

On the weekends, the marines would frequent the bars and often ended up in fistfights. After starting fights, the marines ran back across the street to their barracks. Policemen could not enter the Marine Barracks to arrest them. Captain Edwards, who was in charge of the fifth precinct, instructed the policemen to start arresting the marines for any violation—even throwing cigarettes butts on the street or spitting on the sidewalk. After a couple weekends of this activity, the general in charge requested a meeting with our captain and they worked out an agreement.

If any of the marines got out of control in the bars and ran back to the barracks, the policeman would come to the gate and the officer in charge would identify those involved and turn them over to the police. This calmed things down on 8th Street.

We rotated shifts every week. Working the night shift meant spending a lot of the next day in court. Even though you earned a lot of court time leave, we were so short-handed that it was difficult to take the time off. Changing shifts every week meant that out of three weekends we had two short changes and one long change. Short change meant that you got off work at midnight on Saturday and had to be back on duty at 8:00 a.m. on Sunday, or that you got off work at 4:00 p.m. on Saturday and had to report back at midnight. Long change meant that you got off work at 4:00 p.m. on Saturday and reported back the next day at 4:00 p.m. That was rough on the body because just when you started getting adjusted to one shift, you changed to another shift.

While on the police department, I decided that I wanted to learn how to fly airplanes. As a child, I had been fascinated with airplanes and I thought that it was a good time to start taking lessons at an airport in Maryland. My introductory flight took place at Rose Valley Airport. I have difficulty trying to describe what an exhilarating and breathtaking feeling I had during this first flight.

I was hooked on flying and I went on to obtain the following pilot licenses and ratings: Private Pilot License with a Single Engine Rating, Commercial Pilot License with Single Engine and Multi-Engine Ratings, Instrument Pilot License, Flight Instructor License, Instrument Instructor License, and Ground Instructor License. I taught flying for twenty years at P. G. Airpark in Friendly, Maryland, on a part-time basis.

Joe with Sue's mother Myrtle Harper after a sightseeing flight around D.C. and Baltimore

Education:

In 1976, I graduated from the 105th Session of the FBI National Academy in Quantico, Virginia. Law enforcement officials from all around the world were in attendance. I still have contact with some of them. There is a bond that lasts forever among the classmates. I have benefitted from this experience throughout my career with the Secret Service and afterward.

Everywhere I went on assignment, I had someone from that jurisdiction that I could call upon to assist me in our operation. After graduating from the FBI Academy, I was sent by the Secret Service to Penn State University in College Station, Pennsylvania, where I graduated from their Police Executive Development Institute. In 1962, I had graduated from the University of Maryland Law Enforcement Institute in College Park, Maryland. I also received an associate degree in criminal justice from Virginia Western Community College.

The Cuban Missile Crisis

In 1962, Russia placed missiles in Cuba. The United States was able to spot them with U-2 spy planes that took photographs of the sites.

President Kennedy confronted Nikita Khrushchev, secretary of the Communist Party of the Soviet Union, and a stalemate followed.

I was detailed from the Metropolitan Police Department to the White House to assist the White House Police (now called the United States Secret Service Uniformed Division). I was there for three weeks during the crisis. Late one night, I saw—through the windows of the Oval Office—the president, his National Security staff, and military leaders, all huddled around his desk discussing the Cuban situation.

President Kennedy decided to place a naval blockade around Cuba and the Russians threatened to run the blockade. Russia sent ships loaded with missiles toward the blockade. Tensions were running high on both sides. At the last minute, the Russians called off their attempt to run the blockade. They agreed to remove the missiles from Cuba if the United States would remove its missiles from Turkey. Both sides gave up something.

Years later, through news interviews with some of the Russian military leaders, it was confirmed that the Kremlin had given the military commander on the ground in Cuba the authorization to fire nuclear missiles on the United States if we tried to bomb the missile sites in Cuba.

At the time, I did not realize just how close our country had come to a nuclear war. Later, it became clear that a catastrophe had been averted.

Transfer to the White House Police

After the Cuban Missile Crisis, I returned to my assignment with the Metropolitan Police Department. Thereafter, each time a head of state from another country came to Washington, I was detailed to the White House. The Secret Service asked me to transfer over to the White House since I was there so often, and I decided to take them up on the offer. In comparing the working conditions between the Metropolitan Police and the White House Police, there was no hesitation on my part. I felt as if I'd died and gone to heaven."

After transferring over to the White House, I was surprised that they would also allow me to transfer my six weeks of court time leave from the Metropolitan Police. I had already determined that all the leave I had built up was lost, but I considered it worth the change. At that time, the Metropolitan Police were under the federal system and everything was transferable.

Chapter 7

My Career with the Secret Service

Over my twenty years with the Secret Service, I was assigned to different details. I served six presidents (Kennedy, Johnson, Nixon, Ford, Carter, and Reagan). Some of my assignments included the White House Division, USSS Training Division, Foreign Missions Division in Washington and New York, and the Vice President Detail where I was in charge of the Uniformed Division's Detail during the vice presidencies of Walter Mondale and George H. W. Bush.

The Secret Service had been given the responsibility to provide protection for foreign embassies and missions in the United States. We recruited a large number of people to meet this goal.

I was assigned to the Secret Service Training Division as an instructor and one of the courses I taught was "Courtroom Procedures." During the training period, the new officers were taken to the Federal Courthouse where they would observe a trial in session. On one occasion, I had about twenty-five recruits witnessing a trial. During the trial, I stepped out of the courtroom to check on another trial that the recruits could attend. While doing this, the judge took a recess and sent the bailiff out to get me. He approached and said that the judge wanted to see me in his chambers. As we were proceeding to the judge's chamber, I was thinking about what the recruits might have done for the judge to send the bailiff for me. After entering the judge's chamber, he inquired as to who we were and what we were doing in his courtroom. I explained who we were and asked if the group had disturbed the trial. The judge said, "No. On the contrary, I have not seen a better looking and well behaved group and I wanted to know who they are."

We proceeded back to the courtroom and everyone was seated. Before the trial resumed, the judge stated to the attorneys that he wanted to address the court. I was surprised when he asked me to approach the bench. The judge introduced me to the court and had the recruits stand. He told those in the courtroom who we were and proceeded to welcome them to his court and gave a quick rundown on what was expected of them when they would bring their own cases before the court. That turned out to be much better training than we could give them in a classroom.

Comments about the presidents that I served under: President John F. Kennedy

President Kennedy was always pleasant to be around. He was friendly to each of us that provided security for him and his family. President Kennedy was very close to his brothers and sisters. Their families came to the White House often, and there were several touch football games played on the South Lawn.

Mrs. Kennedy was not as friendly as the president and ignored us most of the time. Otherwise, Mrs. Kennedy's taste was excellent in making major decoration changes to the staterooms of the White House (Green Room, Blue Room, and the Red Room). Silk material was placed on the walls of each of these staterooms with new drapes. Also, the drapes in the State Dining Room and the East Room were changed.

When President Kennedy was assassinated, I was working at the White House. All days off and leave were canceled and everyone was on twelve-hour shifts. I was assigned the night shift. When the president's body was brought back to the White House, my assignment was to remain with the casket in the East Room and not let anyone except Mrs. Kennedy near it. About two o'clock one morning, Mrs. Kennedy brought the Catholic bishop of Washington in and had me open the casket for the bishop so that he could give the Catholic Last Rites to President Kennedy. To my knowledge, that was the only time the casket was opened for viewing.

I've already mentioned some facts about President Kennedy. There is much more I could say, but I would like to share a story about his son, John Jr. He was called John John. When he was about two years old, I was standing outside the south entrance to the White House that the First Family used to enter and exit. John John, along with his nurse, came out of the building and walked up to me. He grabbed me by the leg, and started weaving in and out between both legs. He stopped and looked up at me with his big bright eyes and asked, "Got any gum?" His nurse gave me a mean look and said, "Don't you dare give him gum." John John continued weaving in and out between my legs and the nurse eventually led him off for a walk in the south grounds.

Needless to say, I was saddened and had a heavy heart when John Jr. was killed in a plane crash in 1999.

President Lyndon B. Johnson

President Johnson and family

President Johnson was sworn into office after the assassination of President Kennedy. He and the Johnson family continued to live in their private residence in northwest Washington for a couple of months until Mrs. Kennedy could move out of the White House. I was assigned to his private residence. Luci, his younger daughter, was in high school. She had friends over for visits and they often tried to sneak Luci out by having her lie down in their car as they departed with a coat covering her. I stopped the car as they tried to exit and made Luci get out and go back inside the residence. Needless to say, I was not her favorite security person.

During the winter of 1963, I was assigned to the president's private residence. The neighbor brought hot coffee and doughnuts over for those of us standing out in the cold. This nice lady was Shirley Temple Black. I did not recognize her because I had only seen her in the movies when she was a child. She did not make an issue of this and never introduced herself, but we learned who she was. In case there is someone not familiar with her, it is the same Shirley Temple who starred in movies and TV as a child. She later became the US Ambassador to two countries and served as the chief of protocol in the State Department. I understand she is now living in Northern California.

President Johnson was quite a character. He would walk up to a door that was closed and start kicking it and cursing, demanding to know why it was not open. He was about six foot four, and would not reach down to open the door himself, but waited impatiently for someone else to do it.

Here is another incident with President Johnson. I'm not sure who nicknamed him "Clyde" or why, but when he moved around the White House, we would let the next person along the way know that he was coming. One day he came down the elevator from the family living quarters and started toward the Oval Office in the West Wing. As he exited the mansion, I called ahead to the next person and said, "Clyde is coming." President Johnson, who had just turned the corner, immediately stepped back and said, "I want you to know that my name is not Clyde." He then proceeded to his office.

It was not unusual to be working one of the outer gates at the White House when the phone would ring and a big booming voice would say, "This is Lyndon and I have so-and-so coming in to see me." Any other president would never have done this himself, but "Lyndon" wasn't always patient enough to wait for an aide to do it.

Lady Bird Johnson was a true lady. She was very easy to work with. I worked the weddings of both Lynda Johnson, when she and Chuck Robb were married at the White House, and Luci Johnson, when she married Pat Nugent at the Catholic Shrine of Immaculate Conception in Washington.

Lady Bird Johnson had personal friends visit the White House and, on several occasions, she requested that I give them a tour of the White House.

President Johnson had his brother, Sam Houston Johnson, stay in the White House so an eye could be kept on him. Sam was a person that would speak freely and could be an embarrassment to the president.

Military Draft and Deferments

I was twenty-three when the United States Draft Board called me to come take a physical for the military. I took the physical at Fort Holabird in Baltimore, but President Kennedy requested that I not be drafted because I was needed more at the White House—and I was deferred. During the Johnson administration, I received another notice to report for a physical. Again, after taking the physical, President Johnson wrote a letter to the draft board saying that I was needed at the White House—and I was again deferred. This happened two more times before the draft board stopped notifying me to report.

About a month after one of the deferments by President Johnson, I received a request to ferry a military twin engine aircraft (Cessna 337 Skymaster) from the Cessna factory in Wichita, Kansas, to Saigon, South Vietnam. The Secret Service requested that I be granted a leave of absence for one month to fly the plane there for the military to use on spotter missions. Mine was one of ten planes scheduled to be sent and we would all be flying together.

President Johnson approved the request. I was so excited about this round-the-world trip. We would fly to Newfoundland, Canada, where additional fuel tanks would be installed for the trip across the Atlantic Ocean. From Newfoundland, the next stop would be Reykjavik, Iceland. The next stop was to be Shannon Airport in Ireland, and then we would spend the night in London. The next stop was Paris for a night and then on to Rome. From Rome, our next stop was Ankara, Turkey. From Ankara, we were to fly down the Persian Gulf into the Arabian Sea and across to Bombay, India. Then we were to fly across India to Calcutta. From Calcutta, we were to fly down the Bay of Bengal to Bangkok, Thailand. From Bangkok, we were to fly through the Gulf of Siam and around to Saigon, South Vietnam. After turning the planes over to the military in Saigon, we were to board a commercial airline for the trip back to Washington. There were scheduled stops in Manila, the Philippines, Honolulu, and San Francisco—and finally we were to arrive back at Dulles Airport near Washington, D.C.

After all the planning, and just one week prior to departure, the Pentagon decided not to send the planes. Boy, was I disappointed.

I missed the Johnsons after they left the White House.

President Richard M. Nixon

President Nixon

President Nixon had a photographic memory. Once he met you, he never forgot your name. He showed respect to employees of the White House. During the Christmas to New Year Congressional vacations, he usually spent time in Key Biscayne, Florida. He was so considerate of the agents assigned with him, and not wanting them to be away from their families during the Christmas and New Year holidays, that he would pay from his own money for the spouses to be flown down to Florida and for their lodging.

I was also assigned to work on the wedding detail of Patricia (Tricia) Nixon to Edward Cox at the White House.

Tricia Nixon/Edward Cox wedding

President Nixon and Pat Nixon

There was a lot of unrest in the country during the Johnson and Nixon administrations. During the Johnson administration, he had the Vietnam War and the assassination of Dr. Martin Luther King to deal with. These caused riots all across the country, including Washington. I remember looking out from the White House and seeing parts of the city burning. Even today, I see the images of fires from the riots. The last time I was in Washington and drove up 7th Street and Georgia Ave, there were still burned out buildings.

During the Nixon administration, the Vietnam War brought many protest marches to Washington. Also, there were problems with Iranian students in this country demonstrating against the Shah. The Shah came to Washington many times and, during one of his visits, President Nixon greeted him on the South Lawn of the White House. There were large demonstrations on the Ellipse area just outside the South Lawn. The demonstrators became violent and the police used tear gas on the crowd. The wind was blowing toward the White House and President Nixon and the Shah both were gassed. We had to rush both inside the White House and turn off the air conditioning so that the tear gas did not spread throughout the White House.

There was another incident with the demonstrations by the Iranian students against the Shah. I was assigned to a SWAT team covering this demonstration. The same group, in the past, had become violent. We were on standby behind the shrubbery, just outside the South Entrance of the White House, when one member of the team accidently pulled the pin of a tear gas grenade. The air conditioning for the White House again had to be shut down.

After the first time the Iranian demonstrators became violent, it was quite a sight to see the police bring in buses and park them bumper to bumper all the way around the White House. A person could not walk between the buses. It worked well, and the United States Park Police brought in policemen on horses. This also worked well because those students did not want to be stepped on by the horses.

My wife was concerned about my safety on many occasions. This incident with the Iranian's was especially so when she saw on TV the demonstrators using rocks and big pieces of wood as weapons against the police.

President Nixon was forced to resign during the Watergate controversy because of faulty decisions made by his staff and the resulting political consequences. Earlier, Vice President Spiro Agnew had resigned due to legal problems that went back to when he was governor of Maryland.

VP Spiro Agnew

President Nixon had appointed Gerald Ford to the position and he was approved by the United States Senate.

President Gerald R. Ford

President Gerald Ford

When President Nixon resigned, Vice President Gerald Ford was sworn in as president. He was the first vice president and president not elected by the people. After he became president, Nelson Rockefeller took his place as vice president—also by appointment.

There were two attempted assassinations of President Ford, both by women. These attempts took place in California. The first was by Lynette "Squeaky" Fromme, on September 5, 1975, and the second was by Sara Jane Moore, on September 22, 1975. Since the death of President Ford, both women have been paroled from prison after serving more than thirty years. I have no idea why these two assassination attempts were made by women. One reason could have been because President Ford pardoned President Nixon over the Watergate scandal. If you look back over history, you will find that most attempts are made by men.

I was with Vice President Nelson Rockefeller when Sara Jane Moore attempted to assassinate President Gerald Ford. I was one of the people that informed Vice President Rockefeller about the incident and was with him when he made his announcement to the press. Sara Jane Moore did get a shot off, but missed. A marine, Oliver Sipple, hit her arm, causing the second shot to miss. This almost created a situation where we could have had two presidents that were not elected by the people since Vice President Rockefeller had been appointed to the office after Gerald Ford replaced President Nixon upon his resignation.

President Jimmy Carter

President Jimmy Carter

President Jimmy Carter was elected to office in 1976. He served from 1977 to 1981. Early in his administration, President Carter reluctantly allowed the Shah of Iran—after his government had been overthrown—to enter the United States for medical treatment. He moved around hospitals in New York and Texas before returning to Egypt where he died of complications from his surgery in the United States. He is buried in Egypt. This was also when the Iranians overran the US Embassy in Tehran, Iran, and took embassy employees hostage.

In September 1979, I was sent to New York to set up a detail to cover heads of state attending the opening of the United Nations General Assembly. While in the process of setting up our command post in a Midtown Manhattan hotel, I received a telephone call from my superior in the White House who informed me that he had a handwritten note from President Carter wanting to know why I needed touch tone phones in New York. This new technology was required in order for the detail to have secure communications with the White House. President Carter was concerned with the additional cost that would be incurred. I called the phone company and had the phones removed. The president did not realize that this would decrease the communications between New York and the White House. When I returned to the White House, the subject never came up.

President Carter taught a Sunday school class at First Baptist Church of Washington about six blocks from the White House at 16th and O streets, N.W. When the president attended church, it usually created some disruption, but we tried to keep it to a minimum.

President Carter had his brother Billy stay at the White House due to his beer drinking and talking to the press. An agent was assigned to him to make sure that he didn't get into trouble. The Carter administration was embarrassed when Billy visited Libya and then registered as a foreign agent for Libya. He then received a large loan from Libya. Needless to say, Billy was a colorful person. One example of his outlandish public behavior was when he urinated on an airport runway in full view of the press. Billy died on September 25, 1988, at fifty-one from pancreatic cancer.

After President Carter was defeated by Ronald Reagan in the 1980 election, he moved back to Georgia. He bought a summer home in Ellijay, Georgia (Sue's hometown). While he was living there, he taught a Sunday school class at the First Baptist Church of Ellijay.

Also, after leaving office, he often traveled up and down Interstate 81 and would spend the night in Roanoke, Virginia. He always stayed at the Days Inn because he was a close friend of the corporate owner. At the time, I was working at the Marriott Hotel in Roanoke, and the Secret Service agents accompanying him would call and ask me to get rooms at the Marriott for the agents not needed at the Days Inn.

I feel fortunate to have been selected to be in charge of the detail at the vice president's residence. I had a great working relationship with Vice Presidents Mondale and Bush—as well as with Mrs. Mondale and Mrs. Bush.

Bill Mondale was in high school while his father was vice president. Bill was a free spirit. There was never a dull moment when he was around. The Mondales were often out of town and depended on us to make sure he didn't get into trouble.

Vice President and Mrs. Joan Mondale invited Sue and me to the Vice President's Residence for some social functions.

Sue, VP Mondale, Joan Mondale & Joe

Joan Mondale, VP Mondale, Sue & Joe

Joe with Joan Mondale at the VP Christmas Party, 1979

President Ronald Reagan

President Ronald Reagan

It was so easy to work with President Ronald Reagan. He showed the same graciousness to his staff that he demonstrated to the public on television.

On March 30, 1981, John Hinckley, Jr. attempted to assassinate President Reagan outside a Washington hotel. He was found not guilty by reason of insanity and has remained under institutional psychiatric care since then. President Reagan was rushed to George Washington Hospital where he underwent emergency surgery to remove the bullet. The Emergency Powers Act is when the president is incapacitated and he relinquishes his duties to the vice president. This act was not initiated on this occasion.

During the attempted assassination of President Reagan, I was assigned to the vice president's detail.

Even though I was in charge of the vice president's residence detail, from time to time I would travel on trips with President Reagan. I would do the advance planning with federal, state, and local law enforcement agencies.

One day, Vice President George H. W. Bush walked into my office at the vice president's residence and asked if I would take a walk with him. We walked through the grounds of the Naval Observatory talking about things in general.

He said, "Joe, do you think it would be okay if my personal vehicle could be parked inside the residence grounds?"

I said, "Sure, Mr. Vice President, any time you want to bring it in, just let us know which car it is."

He pointed to a vehicle parked in the Naval Observatory grounds and said, "There it is."

I said, "That is Mr. So-and-So's car."

He said, "No, that's my car, and he just drives it for me."

I apologized and made sure that his car would be permitted to drive inside the grounds and park by the residence.

Vice President Bush was such a gentleman. He was always very gracious in requests of the Secret Service personnel. He respected our authority with matters of security.

I retired from the United States Secret Service in 1982. President Reagan gave me a large plaque in the shape of a shield with a bronze bust of each of the six presidents that I had served. In the middle of the plaque is a bronze plate containing a letter from him, which commended me for my service to the country and congratulated me on my retirement.

This plaque is a prized possession of mine. I feel honored to have received it.

Joe's Retirement Plaque from President Reagan

George H.W, & Barbara Bush

Joe & Barbara Bush at Joe's Retirement

Barbara Bush

Joe & Barbara Bush at Joe's Retirement

Vice President Bush had me bring my family to meet with him in his office where pictures were taken and he gave each of us a gift. The White House Photo Office, who took the pictures, somehow lost that roll of film and we never received the pictures. I was disappointed, but I think Sue and the boys were more so. Barbara Bush gave me a retirement party at the vice president's residence.

Four presidents at the White House in 1981 enroute to the funeral of Pres. Anwar Sadat of Egypt

There were many occasions when I worked long hours with no days off. On out of town assignments, I routinely worked sixteen- to eighteen-hour days, especially during presidential campaigns. Once in New York covering heads of state who were there to address the United Nations General Assembly, the Secret Service sent the deputy director and assistant directors up to try to lift our spirits. They advised us that the director was requesting Congress to let him hire more people so that we would not have to be away from home so much and for such long periods of time. The additional manpower never came about.

I was in management positions the last twelve years of my career with the Secret Service. I was fortunate to have provided protection for kings, queens, presidents, prime ministers, and many other dignitaries. I even provided protection for Pope John Paul II on his visit to Washington. Before departing, he came by and shook hands with our detail.

VP Mondale, Pope John Paul II and Joe Dye

There was an incident with a helicopter at the White House. I was assigned to the vice president's residence one night when a member of the military who had washed out of flight school stole a helicopter from one of the military bases in the Washington area. He flew it around Washington for some time while being chased by other military and police helicopters and then approached the White House. As it approached the south grounds, the Uniformed Division personnel opened gunfire on it, forcing it to land on the south grounds. The pilot was arrested and turned over to the military. The next day, I was at the White House and saw the helicopter being prepared by the military for its removal. To this day, I do not know how the pilot survived the incident because the helicopter was riddled with bullet holes. The pilot had only been hit in the leg.

On January 13, 1982, I had been flying in one of the United States Park Police helicopters and had completed our patrol of the Washington area. It had been snowing for several hours and the streets were becoming hazardous. We worked very closely with the Park Police and occasionally rode along to observe certain areas that might be of interest to our security.

Shortly thereafter, I went off duty and was headed home when I heard on the radio that an Air Florida flight taking off from National Airport had crashed into the Potomac River by the 14th Street Bridge. I had just passed the Pentagon and was not caught up in all the traffic that had developed. By this time, the snow was coming down heavily and traffic on all routes out of Washington was at a standstill.

After getting home, I saw on TV that the helicopter that I had been on was picking people out of the frozen Potomac River. My wife was caught in the traffic as she traveled across the 14th Street Bridge and she could see the plane in the river. The plane had come down on the bridge and crushed several vehicles, killing some of the occupants. Sue happened to come along later and could not move either way for hours. It took several hours before she could get home. We did not have cell phones then and had no way of contacting each other so I did not know what was happening with her. I had several anxious hours waiting for her to get home.

When I was assigned to the Foreign Missions Division, I had contact with all the embassies in Washington. We protected the embassies—some more than others, depending on the situation with each. The Russian Embassy was always a hot spot and often had demonstrations by the Jewish Defense League (JDL). In Washington, there is a law banning demonstrations within five hundred feet of an embassy. The JDL would push the limit on this and I had to enforce the law. They filed many suits with the courts claiming their rights were being violated. The Secret Service Legal Office handled these complaints most of the time without me knowing about them. When I retired, our legal office gave me a large file of all the suits filed by the JDL concerning me. I did not realize that I had been named in so many suits. All the cases were dismissed by the court without me even knowing about most of them.

I retired from the Secret Service in 1982 and moved to Roanoke. In Roanoke, I worked for Virginia Western Community College, Marriott Hotels, the Virginia Department of Criminal Justice, and the Hotel Roanoke. I am now fully retired.

After moving to Roanoke, Sue began working at the Veterans Affairs Administration Hospital in Salem, Virginia, as a contracting specialist. She retired from the VA in December 1997.

Chapter 8

Religion in My Life

All my life, I have been involved in church activities. As far back as I can remember, my mother would take my brothers, sisters, and me to Valley View Freewill Baptist Church in Hickory Junction. My father did not attend church until I was about nine years old. He accepted Christ as Lord and Savior and was baptized in Lewis Creek. He then became very active in the church.

Clarence Dye being baptized

BAPTISMAL CERTIFICATE

This Certifies that

In obedience to the command and in imitation of the example of our Lord Jesus Christ

Joe Dye

was "buried with Him in baptism" on the 26 day of Sept. 1954 at [illegible] Va

Date of Birth.

No. 8440 © The Stand. Pub. Co., Cin., O. Printed in U. S. A.

Joe's Baptismal Certificate

I accepted Christ as my Lord and Savior when I was a freshman in high school and was also baptized in Lewis Creek.

After moving to Washington, I joined Congress Heights Baptist Church in southeast Washington and became an active member. I taught third grade boys in Sunday school. Congress Heights Baptist Church has since dissolved and the property was sold.

While working at the White House, I was among a few employees that formed a Bible study and prayer group. President Johnson allowed us to use the Roosevelt Room across the hall from the Oval Office. We would meet each Wednesday morning. I attended most of the meetings, but occasionally my work assignments would interfere. The Secret Service did not object to me attending, but actually encouraged me.

On April 24, 1964, Sue and I were married at Metropolitan Baptist Church on Capitol Hill. Sue was already a member of this church and was working there as a secretary. I moved my church membership to Metropolitan Baptist Church and we remained active as leaders with the youth group.

Joe & Sue's Wedding Reception

Sue went back to work for the federal government. First, she assisted a Presidential Commission on Government Procurement. She then transferred to the General Services Administration as a budget analyst. In 1967, we purchased our first house in Dale City, Virginia, and moved our church membership to First Baptist Church of Woodbridge, Virginia. A few months later, Dale City Baptist Church was formed and we were among the first members. We met in the Woodbridge High School until a building could be constructed in Dale City. I was ordained a deacon in the Dale City Baptist Church. We later moved to Springfield, Virginia, and joined the First Baptist Church of Springfield. We were active there for the twelve years before my retirement.

During Nixon's administration, he started having ministers come into the White House to conduct services. Sue and I were invited to attend one conducted by Dr. Norman Vincent Peale.

WHITE HOUSE WORSHIP SERVICE

Sunday, January 21, 1973

We were also invited to attend some of the Presidential Prayer Breakfasts, usually held in one of the large hotels in Washington.

Since moving to Roanoke in 1982, we have been active in the First Baptist Church of Roanoke. I am currently serving on the Church Board of Directors, the Fellowship of Deacons, the Church Council, and the Church Endowment Committee of which I am chairman. Sue and I serve as directors of the Seniors Ministry (55+ Ministry) and we work with the third and fourth grade boys in the AWANA program. Sue and I are also leaders in our Life Group (Sunday school).

Chapter 9

Other People Who Have Touched My Life

When Sue first arrived in Washington, she lived in a row house at the corner of Pennsylvania Avenue and 3rd Street, SE, which is three blocks from the Capitol Building. There were several other girls living at that address who attended Metropolitan Baptist Church. One, Helen Bendall, later married John Berry. Over the years, we have been very close. They bought a house in Dale City, and after we moved to Springfield, they bought a house there. We went to the same churches over the years until Sue and I moved to Roanoke.

John and Helen were the owners of a paint and wallpaper store in Annandale, Virginia. After several years of operating the store, they decided to close it. John was hired by the Fairfax County School System and worked there until his retirement.

Helen was hired by Congressman Earl Hutto of Florida to work in his office on Capitol Hill. Congressman Hutto was also a member of First Baptist Church of Springfield. Helen continued to work for Congressman Hutto until he retired from the United States Congress. Helen transferred to the Inspector General's Office for the Pentagon, where she worked until her retirement from the federal government.

After Helen and John retired, they built a house in Helen's hometown of Russellville, Alabama, where they reside today. We continue to visit each other and Helen keeps our former youth group aware of what's going on with each of us. John grew up in Arlington; I think he is still adjusting to the small town life of Russellville. Over the years, we have taken several trips together and continue to enjoy each other's company.

I have lots of items given me by different presidents, such as pens where they signed legislation into law concerning our agency, and wedding missals from Lynda Johnson, Luci Johnson, and Tricia Nixon. Other gifts included jewelry, such as cufflinks, tie clips, money clips, lapel pins, paperweights, and other items. I also have the large framed Christmas cards signed by all the presidents from Kennedy through Reagan and autographed photos of all the presidents I served under except President Kennedy.

In June 2007, Sue and I were visiting family and friends in the Washington area and I asked Sue if she would like to visit the White House. We had not been back in several years. Even though I had been retired for twenty-five years, I remembered some phone numbers at the White House and called to request a tour. I informed the lady that answered the phone who I was and what I wanted to do.

After I talked a little while, she said "Mr. Dye, you don't have to tell me who you are. I was here before you retired and I remember you."

For security reasons, she took all the identification information needed to clear me, my wife, and two other guests. At the White House, we were met at the checkpoint gate and escorted in by a captain of the United States Secret Service Uniformed Division. Inside the White House, I saw several people I had known prior to my retirement. I asked about Gary Walters, the chief usher of the White House. Gary oversaw the operations of the White House and had once been a member of the Uniformed Division of the Secret Service. He later became a Secret Service Agent and then transferred to the Usher's Office where he later became the Chief Usher. Gary met us and told my friends that I was his mentor. I trained Gary when he started working for us. He informed me that there were some other people that he wanted me to meet. He asked me to show my guests around some of the private areas while he found these people.

He said, "You know this place better than I do."

I took that as a compliment and it was good to know that I still knew my way around the place. We later went out on the South Lawn and Gary took a picture of Sue and me standing by the south entrance. While there, the two Bush daughters, Barbara and Jena, came out and said hello as they were departing.

I found that the six presidents I served all had their pluses and minuses. The Secret Service did not get involved with their politics. I found that the presidents usually were easy to work with. Sometimes if we had problems, it was with their staff

One day while waiting at a bus stop, I met Kenneth Henson who had just been discharged from the navy. He was employed by the Library of Congress. We became good friends, and I remember some fishing trips that we made to South Holston Lake near Abingdon, Virginia.

I introduced Ken to Wilma Miller of Flat Rock, Illinois, who was working for the FBI in Washington. Later, I had the privilege to give Wilma to Ken in marriage.

Joe & Wilma Miller at her wedding to Ken Henson

Joe, Doug & Ken

Ken's car and Joe's tent

Joe shaving while camping on South Holston Lake

Later Ken resigned from the Library of Congress and moved to his hometown of Decatur, Alabama. He was hired by the US Post Office in Decatur where he worked until retirement. We have remained good friends throughout the years.

In 1967, after moving into our new house in Dale City, Chuck and Vivian Boling moved in next door. We immediately became friends and continue to be so to this day. Chuck is an avid fisherman and we have enjoyed our times fishing for largemouth bass on the Rappahannock River between Fredericksburg and the Chesapeake Bay. We also fished for bluefish on the Chesapeake Bay.

Chuck Boling

Chapter 10

Vacations

When our boys were small, we vacationed at Smith Mountain Lake, which is about twenty miles east of Roanoke. The first place we rented was at Cedar Keys Cabins on the Bedford County side, near the dam. A fishing boat was included in the rental and I took everyone out fishing. Tim and Brad both liked to put their lines in the same place, which resulted in conflict. I then started taking one of them out at a time; Sue has told me more than once that it saved her sanity. Tim was a late sleeper and Brad got up early so that worked out well with Brad fishing in the early morning and Tim in the evening.

Afterward, I purchased a fifth wheel camper and we liked staying at Crazy Horse Campground at Smith Mountain Lake. We also used the fifth wheel on several vacation trips around the country.

Before retirement, I rented space at Crazy Horse Campground and left the fifth wheel there year round. After moving to Roanoke, I found little time for fishing and camping and sold the camper after a couple years.

Sue's family has owned a 150-acre farm in Gilmer County, Georgia, since the 1840s. Throughout the years, we spent most of our vacation time helping on the farm. We canned lots of vegetables and fruit. When driving back to Washington, I was concerned that a policeman might stop us because our vehicle was so low in the back from the weight of the canned goods.

It was a fourteen-hour drive from Washington to the farm, which made it too long of a trip without stopping for the night. It made the second part too short to not continue so we usually did not stop for the night. After our sons were born, it became much harder to travel because, after thirty minutes, they started asking if were there yet or how much longer it would be. After getting there, everything was all right because the boy's cousins were usually waiting. The cousins—Billy Harper, Brent Harper, Darrell Harper, Kevin Harper and Stephanie Burnett Bowyer—were there about every day. When Billy learned that we were coming, he was there when we arrived and stayed with his grandparents until we left.

Stephanie, Brad Tim & Billy

Brad, Brent, Tim, Darrell & Billy

After Sue's father died, there was a tragic accident on one of our trips to the farm. Fourteen-year-old Billy was using the farm tractor to move a downed tree with Brent. They were coming up an embankment when the tractor turned over, pinning Billy underneath it. Billy was driving and Brent jumped off when it turned over. Billy was dead before we could get the tractor off.

All the other kids were watching as we tried to get the tractor off and I asked Sue to take them to the house to wait. I had Sue call her cousin who lived just down the road to bring his tractor to help. When he arrived, I already had a chain hooked to the overturned tractor and the cousin was able to lift it up enough so I could pull Billy from underneath it. I performed CPR on Billy until the rescue squad arrived, but I knew it was useless because I could see the air going past the lungs and into the stomach. As I expected, his lungs had burst. Needless to say, that was not one of our best vacations.

Over the years, our family has enjoyed vacationing at the beach. We like going to different ones, but there are two that we have visited several times. They are Hilton Head and Myrtle Beaches in South Carolina. Others where we have vacationed in are Ocean City, Maryland, Virginia Beach, Virginia, the Outer Banks and Atlantic Beach, North Carolina, Saint Augustine, Cocoa Beach, and Melbourne Beaches in Florida. We still take the grandchildren to the beach each summer. They look forward to the vacation and love to play in the ocean and build sandcastles on the beach.

Other places we have enjoyed include New England, the Eastern Provinces of Canada, and the US and Canadian Rockies. We love the beauty of the country and people of Canada. Our family has vacationed in Nashville at the Opryland Campground. We attended an FBI National Associates regional meeting at Opryland Hotel. While there, the associates arranged a special performance at the Grand Old Opry just for our group.

The most memorable of our vacations was at the farm in Georgia. Our sons still talk about the good times they had with their cousins, playing in the creek and roaming the countryside. After Sue's parents passed away, the farm was divided among the five family members. Today, Sue's older brother, Franklin, and his son, Kevin, are the only family members living there.

Boat trip from Washington to Florida

In the early 1960s, shortly after transferring to the White House Police, I was asked by John Wheeler, who had just retired from the D. C. Transit System, to help him take a newly purchased cabin cruiser boat from Washington to Clearwater, Florida, where he and his wife, Glady, were moving. We started out with four people on board, Mr. and Mrs. Wheeler, a friend of theirs, and me. The friend of the Wheelers and Mrs. Wheeler went as far a Norfolk before returning to Washington. Mrs. Wheeler took a bus to Clearwater and Mr. Wheeler and I continued the trip with the boat. Mr. Wheeler requested my help because of my knowledge of navigation. He was not experienced with boating. I used two weeks of leave for the trip.

It took an entire day to travel down the Potomac River from Washington to the Chesapeake Bay. The second day was on the Chesapeake Bay to Norfolk, Virginia. The Chesapeake Bay was the roughest part of the trip. We had eight-to-ten-foot waves coming from the rear, and when the waves struck the stern, it threw the rear of the boat with the rudder and propeller out of the water, leaving us with no control. The boat would be turned sideways, and then another wave would strike us from the side, tossing us around like a rag doll. After the rudder and propeller were back in the water, we could straighten the boat, but it wasn't long before another wave would hit us from behind. We were tossed around until the rudder and propeller settled back into the water. No one panicked during the rough ride, but Mr. and Mrs. Wheeler experienced seasickness. I'm sure that had a bearing on her decision to get off in Norfolk. It was a relief to enter Hampton Roads and dock in Norfolk for the night.

Since I had always heard how rough the Gulf of Mexico could get, little attention had been given to the Chesapeake Bay during our planning. The third day, we traveled through the Great Dismal Swamp Canal, located between Suffolk, Virginia, and the North Carolina border. I found it interesting to navigate the locks on the Intercoastal Waterway. These locks were very small compared to the ones on the Erie Canal and the Panama Canal. Crossing the Albemarle Sound on the eastern shore of North Carolina was a little rough due to that body of water being so shallow that the wind causes it to get rough in a short period of time. From North Carolina to the Florida border, the distance between marinas created a problem of having enough fuel to make it from one to another. We ran out of fuel once and the Coast Guard had to come and tow us to the next marina. We lowered the anchor and the boat was dead in the water for a couple hours after we called the Coast Guard for assistance. Any time the Coast Guard is called for assistance, they give a thorough inspection of your boat. We did not worry about the inspection because everything was seaworthy.

We spent some time in Charleston, South Carolina, and Savannah, Georgia, before reaching Florida. Charleston and Savannah both are beautiful cities. In Charleston, we took the boat around Fort Sumter and walked around the waterfront. The old mansions in Charleston and Savannah are wonderful reminders of the past.

From the Florida border through the remainder of our trip, there were marinas located very close together. We traveled to Fort Pierce, Florida, and then followed that portion of the Intercoastal Waterway to Lake Okeechobee. We crossed Lake Okeechobee and traveled down the Caloosahatchee River to Fort Myers, Florida, where it emptied into the Gulf of Mexico. As we entered the Gulf of Mexico, there were storm warning flags out, but it was not nearly as rough as the Chesapeake Bay had been. We could see the storm building up to our west and we went out about fifteen miles into the Gulf so that there would be a direct route into Tampa Bay. We were able to stay ahead of the storm and reached Tampa Bay safely and then on to Clearwater.

We traveled the Intercoastal Waterway for most of the journey, but had to venture out into the Atlantic Ocean a few times. The Intercoastal Waterway was established along the coast, usually just inland where boaters have protection from the rough ocean waters. We made several stops along the way, and did not travel at night.

After arriving in Clearwater, I was an usher in Dick and Sally Moore's wedding in Mulberry, Florida. I had met Dick while he was stationed at Bolling Air Force Base in Washington. Dick is now a retired Baptist Minister and has just returned from overseas where he had been serving as a missionary. He is presently living in the Lakeland, Florida, area.

After arriving back in Washington from the boat trip and the wedding, Ken Henson and I went on another weeklong fishing trip to South Holston Lake. Because of all the activities and being away from work for so long, I was ready to get back to work after the trip.

Chapter 11
Flying Adventures

I truly love flying. In the early 1960s, there were several occasions after working the midnightshift as a policeman—and my adrenalin still flowing—I would go out to the airport, rent a plane, and fly to Ocean City, Maryland, to have breakfast. This would be a way to relieve the stress from the night before. It was so peaceful to get up in the air by myself, and fly across the Chesapeake Bay to the eastern shore of Maryland. After having breakfast, I usually would fly about five miles out over the Atlantic Ocean, and then turn around and head back to Washington. By the time I got to my apartment, I would be so relaxed that sleep came easily.

There is another flight I'll never forget. Back in the late 1960s, I was asked by another instructor to take one of his students on an actual instrument flight. The student and I decided to fly from Washington to Raleigh-Durham Airport.

We began at P. G. Airpark, now named Potomac Airport, in Friendly, Maryland. After filing a flight plan via telephone with the Flight Service Station at Washington National Airport, now called Ronald Reagan National Airport, we had thirty minutes to get airborne and activate the plan with Air Traffic Control (ATC), or the flight plan would be cancelled. It was about 8:00 p.m. and the weather was overcast. The cloud ceiling of 1,000 feet required the flight to be made in actual instrument conditions. After takeoff, we were instructed by ATC to remain VFR (Visual Flight Rules) until they could get us cleared and mixed into the traffic. Before getting our clearance from Air Traffic Control, I had difficulty staying below the clouds and clearing some hills that were about six hundred feet in elevation.

After getting our clearance, which included instructions to climb to 6,500 feet and switch radio frequency to the Washington Center, the student took over the controls and we proceeded to execute our flight plan. It is worth noting that, while instrument flying on the East Coast, the traffic was so heavy that you almost always flew under radar contact. Air traffic control was constantly monitoring you and it was not necessary to make position reports along the route.

Everything was going well until just south of Richmond when Washington Center advised us that radar contact was terminated. This practice is common in the wide open spaces of the Midwest where the traffic is light. We continued on our flight plan, but were required to report our position at designated checkpoints. We were in the middle of white clouds and right on schedule, when all a sudden everything turned pitch black. The plane was thrown from side to side and up and down. I took control of the plane and had the student get on the radio and advise Washington Center that we were in a thunderstorm. The altimeter jumped 1,000 feet, which meant that we had hit an updraft. Lightning was flashing, causing a blue flame (static electricity) in a circle around the propeller, and running along the leading edges of both wings where the fuel tanks were located.

We had two radios on board. Each radio was for navigation and communications. The lightning knocked out both radios. We lost all contact with ATC and were blown off course. For what seemed to be an hour, but turned out to be five minutes, I flew back toward our original course. Finally, radio contact with ATC was re-established and I requested a lower altitude to get out of the rough turbulence. The lower altitude didn't help with the turbulence. Washington Center then had us back in radar contact and vectored us to the Raleigh-Durham Airport.

As we continued our descent, it was a wonderful sight to break out of the clouds and see the approach and runway lights straight ahead.

After getting on the ground, I proceeded to the control tower to complain about them allowing me to fly into a thunderstorm. Before I could do much complaining, they advised me that the weather was turning into a stationary front and would remain right over the airport. It was expected to keep the airport closed for about three days. They advised me that within fifteen minutes they were closing the airport to all traffic, and if I wanted to get out, I needed to leave immediately. I filed another flight plan back to Washington and was the last plane to take off before they closed the airport.

The flight back to Washington was uneventful; we climbed through the clouds and broke out on top. There was a full moon—and soft white clouds billowed underneath us. It was about midnight when we approached Washington National Airport and proceeded to fly down the glide slope, which included entering the clouds again. After breaking out of the clouds over the Woodrow Wilson Bridge, I requested permission to break off the approach to National Airport and fly direct to P. G. Airpark. After receiving permission, I proceeded underneath the clouds to P. G. Airpark. On our final approach, I canceled our instrument flight plan with the tower at National Airport and thanked the controller for his assistance before landing. After that experience, I don't believe that student ever returned to flying.

In late winter of 1965, one of our White House Policemen had been back to visit family in his hometown of Latrobe, Pennsylvania, southeast of Pittsburgh, and was killed in an auto accident while en route to Washington.

The White House Police chartered a bus to take about fifty members of the police to Latrobe for his funeral. The day of the funeral, the group departed Washington about 2:00 a.m. I took two other members with me and flew to Latrobe in a small plane, but did not leave until 7:00. I had called the funeral home before leaving Washington to get information about the arrangements and—to my surprise—they informed me that a vehicle would be waiting at the airport for us. We arrived at the Latrobe airport and a limo was waiting for us. The driver advised us that the limo was for the three of us and, after the funeral, we could use it for the remainder of the day. I was uncomfortable with this and made sure that the funeral home was not charging the family for the service.

At the funeral home, the members on the bus were already there. I tried to get our chief and other officials to use the limo, but they refused. After the funeral service, we used the limo to go to the cemetery and then straight to the airport. We were back in Washington by 2:00 p.m.—and the bus with the others did not arrive back until about 7:00 p.m.

In August 1968, I flew Sue, our ten-month-old son, Timothy, and Sue's sister, Mary, from Washington to visit family in Ellijay.

We had to make an emergency landing in Charlottesville. On the cowling of the Beechcraft Bonanza is a small hinged metal door for checking the oil in the engine. The latch on the door came loose while in flight and the door was flapping in the wind. After landing, it was determined that the door had not been damaged. I secured it and the flight was continued.

Family flight to Georgia in 1968

Thunderheads were building up over the Smoky Mountains and I climbed to fifteen thousand feet to stay above the clouds. When you get above ten thousand feet, the oxygen becomes thin. Since we did not have oxygen available on board, I had to descend below the clouds. There was turbulence at that level and the remainder of the trip was quite rough. Sue and Mary both were experiencing airsickness by the time we arrived at Gilmer County Airport, where Sue's father, Frank Harper, was waiting for us.

During our visit in Ellijay, I had to fly to Dalton, Georgia, to refuel the plane, because the Gilmer County Airport did not have the octane-rated fuel required for my plane. Two friends from Ellijay, Bill Reese, the postmaster, and James Holt, the pastor of First Baptist Church of Ellijay, flew with me.

In the early 1970s, I flew my younger brother Doug from Washington to Richlands to attend the funeral in Honaker of our dear friend and neighbor, George Fields. After the funeral, my mother wanted us to stay and have dinner with her before flying back to Washington. We stayed and visited with her and other family members longer than planned so it was about ten o'clock before we left the airport in Richlands. My brother Stanley had called someone who told him that we had left Richlands several hours before we actually did. He called my brother's wife and relayed this information. Doug's wife then called my wife and they both were upset, thinking that something was wrong. After landing at P. G. Airpark, I called Sue to inform her that we were back and would be home shortly. Needless to say, I had to explain what had delayed us on our return trip. I also had a conversation with my brother about calling my sister-in-law before getting the actual facts and causing a stressful situation.

In 2001, I had a heart attack and have given up active flying. The only flying I do now is on commercial airlines, in a flight simulator, or as a ride-along with another pilot.

Chapter 12

My Health and Final Thoughts

I had good health until just before my last retirement. I was fifty-seven years old when I was diagnosed with leukemia (CLL) in 1997. At first, I was scared not knowing what to expect, but my doctor explained what was happening to my body. He explained the treatment options and relieved my fears. He also said that I probably would die from something else. Since then, I have had several series of chemo treatments administered to just maintain. Dr. Jack Hutcheson, my oncologist, advised me that, at that time, there was no cure for leukemia. He would monitor my situation and, when the white blood count gets to a certain point, he would give me chemo treatments to maintain the blood count at a manageable level. I had had several treatments of chemo drugs with no problems, but during one of the last treatments under Dr. Hutcheson, I had a bad reaction from the drug and the treatment was stopped. Shortly afterward, Dr. Hutcheson decided to retire and I switched oncologists to Dr. William Fintel.

My immune system has been compromised and I have to be very careful about infections. In March 2008, I had a respiratory infection; my family doctor had me admitted to the hospital with a white blood count of 119,000. The normal range for the white count is 4,100 to 10,900. They were able to get the white count down to 93,000. Dr. Fintel met with Sue and me and suggested that we consider using

Treanda, a drug that the FDA had just approved for use in the United States. After researching it, we decided to try it. The treatments would consist of two days of treatments followed by twenty-eight days of no treatments; this pattern would continue for six months.

Two weeks after the first set of treatments, testing was done to see if the treatment was working. They had to stop the treatments because the white blood count had dropped to 1,200, which put it in the critically low range. We continued testing my blood for eight months and the white blood count was still below the normal range. Dr. Fintel declared that I was in remission (Praise the Lord!). It has been about eighteen months and my white blood count is still in the good range.

On Sunday, March 2, 2001, Sue and I were getting ready for church. After getting dressed, I walked down our driveway to retrieve the newspaper, but I began feeling lousy while returning to the house. Sue was still in the bathroom getting dressed so I lay down on the bed. Sue said she felt the need to check on me for some reason. When she entered the bedroom, I was unconscious on the bed. She tried to rouse me, but couldn't. She said that my face had already turned blue. There was a phone beside the bed and she called 911. The operator kept her on the phone until the EMS crew arrived.

I remember vaguely waking up enough to know that I was being rolled down our sidewalk and placed in the rescue vehicle. The EMS crew advised Sue that, on the way to the hospital, my heart stopped beating twice and they had to shock me both times to get it beating again. I remember waking up in the operating room with the doctor working on me. I had one artery 100 percent blocked and another one with 90 percent blockage. The doctor performed angioplasty and opened the artery that was completely blocked and placed a stent in the artery. He had me wait four weeks and then did angioplasty on the other artery and placed two stents in it. Since then, my heart has been fine and I have a stress test conducted each year. The FAA has informed me that, since I did not have open heart surgery, I could renew my flight medical certificate and continue flying. I have decided that, at this stage of life, it is not feasible or practical to do so.

There has never been a problem regarding my leg that I had the problem with as a child.

Final Thoughts

My life has been blessed with many wonderful—and some not so wonderful— experiences, but each has allowed me to grow as a person. I thank God for all the blessings that He has given me. Sue and I have been fortunate to have lived in the Washington area for twenty-five years where so many fine people crossed our paths. We have fond memories of Metropolitan Baptist Church and all the wonderful people that made up that church. The youth group was special and its individuals are now scattered all around the world. We have, from time to time, reunions with the group and our adult leaders that are still alive. Reverend John Cochran, who was the minister overseeing the youth at Metropolitan Baptist, and his wife, Mable, have been very special people in our lives. Sue was John's secretary at the church on Capitol Hill in Washington.

When we were married, Sue's father (Frank Harper) was very ill and unable to travel to Washington from Georgia. John substituted for him and walked her down the aisle and gave her in marriage to me. Our families continue to be close friends.

God is good. He has provided for my every need and I trust that He will continue to do so. I realize that every day I have remaining here on earth is a bonus and I want to be doing the Lord's work. Today I cannot do all the things I did when I was young and I get tired easily. My focus in life has changed and I look forward to the Lord's return.

About the Author

Joe Dye started this endeavor as a record of his life history for his children and grandchildren, and it grew into a story that he wanted to share with others. He was born on a farm in southwestern Virginia, in 1940, and as an adult, served Presidents Kennedy through Reagan as a member of the United States Secret Service. Today, Joe enjoys retirement in Roanoke, Virginia, with his wife, Sue, and their family of two sons, two daughters-in-law, and three grandsons.

CPSIA information can be obtained at www.ICGtesting.com
Printed in the USA
245258LV00001B/22/P

9 781462 705177